A SPACE RIDE TO SATURN!

5th Grade Astronomy Book
Children's Astronomy & Space Books

Wouldn't it be great to hop on a spaceship and take a little holiday trip to another planet? People do it in movies, so why can't we? Read on and learn the challenges involved in traveling through space.

DESTINATION SATURN

One day humans will visit Saturn. It's the biggest planet in our solar system, and it has remarkable moons circling it. The moon Titan is covered with clouds, so it must have atmosphere. Enceladus has geysers that throw ice into its atmosphere. Could there be life in the ocean of liquid water under the crust of Enceladus?

No human has been anywhere near Saturn yet. Even our neighbor planets in our solar system are much farther away than anyone has ever travelled. Here's what a tourist to Saturn would have to face.

LEAVING EARTH

The first challenge is leaving Earth itself! We are designed for this planet, so leaving it is hard. Gravity tries to hold you down on your home planet.

To leave the Earth, rockets have to accelerate at speeds over 25,000 miles per hour.

Having a spaceship that can deliver that sort of power without exploding, and that can keep its passengers safe, is very

expensive. The spaceship has to be both lightweight and sturdy, and it has to carry all the fuel and supplies it needs.

SPEED AND TIME

Once you get into Earth orbit, or even leave space on your way to another planet, the journey has only just started. And it's a very long road that would take you to Saturn.

We have sent several spaceships to Saturn with sensors and other scientific devices, and the fastest trip so far took a little bit more than two years. We need better and faster rocket engines for our trip to be much quicker.

Even worse, the trip could be much longer. Both Earth and Saturn are moving around the Sun, and sometimes they are much farther away from each other, so the trip could take six years or even more.

The next problem is that space is not empty. It is mostly empty, but if you run into one of the solid bits--a meteor, a comet, or even some debris left behind by a previous spaceship--the collision can do serious damage to your ship, or possibly destroy it.

First you have to get past the 500,000 or so little bits of junk orbiting the earth. This includes little flecks of paint from satellites and the Space Shuttle to hand tools that astronauts dropped.

Then, for the next two years or more on the way to Saturn, you have to dodge or survive collisions with whatever the Universe sends your way. The scientists will do their best to make your spaceship sturdy, but there is no garage you can take it to for repairs.

The next problem is finding your destination. When you drive around on the Earth, you can use a GPS device to tell you where you are and what turns to take next. The GPS device on the car dashboard uses information from satellites overhead. But when you are travelling away from Earth, much less information is available, and it is available less quickly.

Every spaceship develops a careful flight plan to follow. But to follow it, the spaceship needs to know its route and be able to make constant corrections so what it is actually doing matches what it should be doing.

In a trip of two years, being just one mile off course every day would mean you completely miss your target. The further the spaceship gets from Earth, the harder it is for the guidance system to make sure it is on track.

We are designed to live on Earth. Our earth's atmosphere protects us from most of the cosmic rays and solar wind that would otherwise make it impossible for life to exist on our planet. Read the Baby Professor book *A Giant Shield* to learn more about how the atmosphere protects us.

But when we're on our way to Saturn, we are outside the atmosphere. We'll need a spaceship that protects us from space radiation as well as the Earth's atmosphere does when we're at home. Scientists are working on solutions, including arrays of super-magnets that would deflect the cosmic rays around our spaceship. Let's hope they figure it out before it's time for our trip!

FOOD, WATER, AND SUPPLIES

The shortest trip to Saturn we can make so far takes over two years. That means you have to carry with you over 730 days' worth of food, water, air, books to read, medicine, soap, toothpaste and anything else you might need. It's bad enough to stock a spaceship for just one person, but what if there are five or six of you? Where will you store all the stuff you need?

Although Saturn and its moons have lots of raw materials, there is nothing ready for you to use when you get there. So your spaceship has to be big enough to carry a lot of stuff, and smart enough to recycle everything, from water to proteins to oxygen, to keep you alive and healthy for the whole trip.

PHYSICAL AND MENTAL HEALTH

Here on Earth our bodies work with gravity, and we develop strong muscles to do all the things we want to do. In space there is almost no gravity, and so there is less to work with and it is harder to keep your body in shape. Your body's systems would start to forget how to do all the things they need to do to keep you alive.

While you would grow as much as two inches because there is no gravity to hold you back, your muscles and even your bones might waste away from lack of use. Your heart would have to do less work to pump your blood, so it could get lazy.

When you were done with your long trip--two years out to Saturn, at least two years back, plus the time you spend there as a tourist or a scientist--your heart might not be strong enough any more to deliver blood to your body once you got back to Earth.

There are other problems you might never meet on Earth. For instance, the skin on your feet would get soft and start flaking off because you were not walking on it. And your bladder would not tell you when you needed to urinate, so you would have to have a reminder in your calendar to go to the bathroom every couple of hours to keep you from getting sick inside!

Your spaceship will probably have to provide some sort of artificial gravity to fool your body into thinking it is still on Earth, and provide lots of ways for space travellers to get regular exercise. Otherwise, you might change so much on your trip that, even if you get to Saturn and all the way back to Earth again, you might no longer be able to live on your home planet.

An even greater problem might be having to spend two years or more in a tiny, cramped space with constant danger and little privacy. The safest way to keep you sane during your long trip might be to let you sleep for most of it. This would also save on a lot of food and videos!

THE PROBLEM OF ARRIVING

One of the reasons your trip takes so long is that you spend a lot of it slowing down! You have to arrive at Saturn travelling about the same speed that Saturn and its moons are travelling, or you will either shoot right by your target or crash into it. You don't want either of those things!

The next problem will be how to stay somewhere near where you want to stay. Saturn has many, many small moons, and the gravity of each one will affect your spaceship's orbit. And are you going to just stay in your spaceship, or do you want to explore? If you want to explore, you will need a way to land on one of Saturn's moons and then get back to your spaceship when it's time to leave.

WHAT TO DO WHEN NEAR SATURN

We can barely begin to imagine what we will find when we get to Saturn. We may even find signs of intelligent life!

How will we evaluate what we find? Remember that if we are not in our spaceship or in some sort of colony, we will be in a spacesuit.

Even the best spacesuits are clumsy,
built more to protect us than to let
us do complicated tasks. You'll need
tools that are more like the intelligent

robots of science fiction stories, helpers
that aren't bothered by cosmic rays or
the lack of air to breathe.

But if you make it past all these challenges, you might make discoveries that help us understand how all planets were made. You might even find signs of non-Earth life...even intelligent life!

A GREAT ADVENTURE

We are finding out more and more about our Earth, other planets, the solar system, and the whole universe. Read other Baby Professor books, like Can I Dance on the Moon?, to learn about what lies near at hand and far away.

Visit

BABY PROFESSOR
EDUCATION KIDS

www.BabyProfessorBooks.com
to download Free Baby Professor eBooks and view
our catalog of new and exciting Children's Books